Let's Make an

Egg Drop

by Katie Chanez

NORWOOD HOUSE PRESS

Norwood House Press

For information regarding Norwood House Press, please visit our website at:
www.norwoodhousepress.com or call 866-565-2900.

© 2021 by Norwood House Press.

Hardcover ISBN: 978-1-68450-842-6
Paperback ISBN: 978-1-68404-620-1

LIBRARY OF CONGRESS CATALOGING-IN-PUBLICATION DATA

Names: Chanez, Katie, author.
Title: Let's make an egg drop / Katie Chanez.
Description: Chicago : Norwood House Press, 2021. | Series: Make your own: science experiment! | Includes bibliographical references and index. | Audience: Grades 2-3.
Identifiers: LCCN 2019058382 (print) | LCCN 2019058383 (ebook) | ISBN 9781684508426 (hardcover) | ISBN 9781684046201 (paperback) | ISBN 9781684046263 (ebook)
Subjects: LCSH: Physics--Experiments--Juvenile literature. | Eggs--Experiments--Juvenile literature. | Science--Experiments--Juvenile literature.
Classification: LCC QC33 .C44 2020 (print) | LCC QC33 (ebook) | DDC 530.071--dc23
LC record available at https://lccn.loc.gov/2019058382
LC ebook record available at https://lccn.loc.gov/2019058383

328N—072020
Manufactured in the United States of America in North Mankato, Minnesota.

Contents

A raw egg can break when it is dropped. There are ways to protect an egg from cracking.

CHAPTER 1

All about Egg Drops

People do not normally drop things on purpose. But some people do purposely drop eggs. They make carriers for the eggs. They want to see how changing the carrier affects the falling egg. They try to keep the eggs from breaking. Many schools hold egg drop competitions. Competitors create a carrier that will protect an egg from a fall. Some competitions test whose egg can survive the highest drop. Others see who can create a carrier with the fewest pieces. Many of the **forces** acting on the egg affect other falling objects as well. People can use their knowledge of these forces to protect other falling objects.

You will make your own egg drop carrier. To protect the egg, you must understand the forces that are acting upon it. The egg falls to the ground when you let go. This happens because **gravity** pulls it down. Gravity is a force between two objects. Larger objects have a greater pull on smaller objects. Earth has a strong pull. This is what keeps you from floating away into space.

An egg sitting on a table has **potential energy**. Potential energy is energy stored inside an object. The amount of stored energy depends on the object's position. Objects that are high up have a

Apples hanging on a tree have potential energy. Gravity causes them to fall to the ground.

lot of potential energy. These objects are far from the ground. This means gravity has more potential to act on the objects if they fall. An egg on a ladder has more potential energy than an egg on the ground. This is because the egg on the ground is closer to Earth's center of gravity. It cannot fall. The egg on the ladder is farther from Earth's center of gravity. It has greater potential energy because it can move to the ground. When an egg falls, its potential energy turns into **kinetic energy**. This is the energy of moving objects. Pushing the egg off the ladder allows it to move toward the ground.

The egg gains speed as it falls. The egg's speed is its **velocity**. Velocity increases with distance. The higher the egg is when it falls, the faster its velocity is when it hits the ground. An egg dropped from a table will have a slower final velocity than one dropped from a tall building.

The egg would fall forever if it could. This is because of the first law of motion. This law says that an object in motion will stay in

Car airbags protect passengers from impact force.

motion until another force acts upon it. When the egg hits the ground, it creates an **impact** force. This force stops the egg. The faster the egg is falling, the stronger the force is when it hits the ground. It is

An open parachute creates more drag. Drag slows the skydiver to a safe landing speed.

the impact force that breaks the egg. You will need to find a way to protect the egg from the impact force.

One way to keep the egg safe is to increase **drag**. Gravity pulls the egg down. Air pushes back as the egg falls. The air's force is drag.

But the egg continues to fall because gravity's pull is stronger than the drag. Adding drag can slow the egg's speed. You can see this with skydivers. Skydivers fall quickly when they first jump out of a plane. Then they open a parachute. The parachute increases the amount of drag pushing back. This slows skydivers down. Then they can land safely.

Another way to protect the egg is to increase the time of the **collision**. The amount of impact force depends on the weight of the object and how far it falls. The moment the egg hits the ground is nearly instant. Almost all the force hits the egg at once. But if the collision takes longer, the force spreads out more. The collision can be slowed by a few parts of a second. This lessens the force that hits the egg. You can feel this when you jump up and down. Landing with your legs straight will create a strong force. This can hurt. If you bend your knees, the collision takes longer. There is less force on your body. Padding can also increase the time of the collision. This is why many sports require athletes to wear protective pads.

The position of the egg can affect whether it breaks. People crack the sides of an egg when cooking. They do this because the sides break more easily than the ends. The narrow tip is the strongest part of an egg's shell. The oval shape sends force evenly across the rest of the shell. An egg that lands on its tip is less likely to break than an egg that lands on its side.

Forces When Falling

Drag

Gravity

A small basket could be a good option for an egg drop carrier.

CHAPTER 2

Make Your Own Egg Drop

Egg drop competitions are all about finding ways to keep the impact force from breaking an egg. These competitions use materials that you can often find around your home. Sometimes these competitions have extra rules. Some do not allow parachutes or wings. Others do not allow boxes or certain kinds of padding. You can use any materials you like for your egg drop carrier. Ask an adult to check that your materials are OK to use.

To start, you need something to hold the egg. You can make your own carrier using craft materials. Or you could use something premade, such as a box, bag, or cup. You do not want your egg to be able to move around too much. Otherwise, it could fall out of your carrier. Part of your carrier could also accidentally break your egg.

You can stuff materials into your carrier to hold your egg in place. Bubble wrap, paper towels, or other soft materials work well as padding. Padding can keep the egg safe. The padding absorbs force placed on the carrier. Padding can also slow down the collision. It can reduce the amount of impact force. Your padding should be flexible to absorb the impact. Materials like sponges, cotton balls, and bubble wrap work well.

Bubble wrap cushions breakable items. It reduces the impact force.

You can make a carrier with items such as popsicle sticks or straws. The straws make a sort of cage around the egg. This structure can keep the egg from moving. You can even add longer straws to the outside of this. The longer straws act like padding. They will break. This reduces the amount of impact force on the egg.

Increasing drag also reduces the impact force on your egg. The best way to increase drag is to add **surface area**. If there is more surface area, more drag can act on your carrier. Parachutes add surface area when they open. You can add surface area by creating wings or building a wide carrier.

This experiment is best done outside. Broken eggs can make a big mess. Make sure you ask an adult to help you find the best place to drop eggs. Placing newspapers or a tarp on the ground makes the mess easier to clean up. Ask an adult for help if you want to drop your egg from a high place such as a ladder.

Materials Checklist

- ✓ Eggs
- ✓ Glue or tape
- ✓ Scissors
- ✓ String
- ✓ Boxes

- ✓ Plastic bags
- ✓ Plastic cups
- ✓ Bubble wrap
- ✓ Coffee filters
- ✓ Cotton balls

- ✓ Straws
- ✓ Paper
- ✓ Newspaper or tarp
- ✓ Crayons or pencils

19

You may come up with several ideas before you have one you like. Try drawing some out on paper.

CHAPTER **3**

Science Experiment!

Now that you know what keeps an egg from breaking, put your knowledge to use and make a carrier that keeps it safe!

1. Take a few minutes to **brainstorm** ideas for ways to keep your egg safe. Will your carrier increase drag? Or will it slow down the collision? Can you combine both methods? You can write down or draw your ideas.

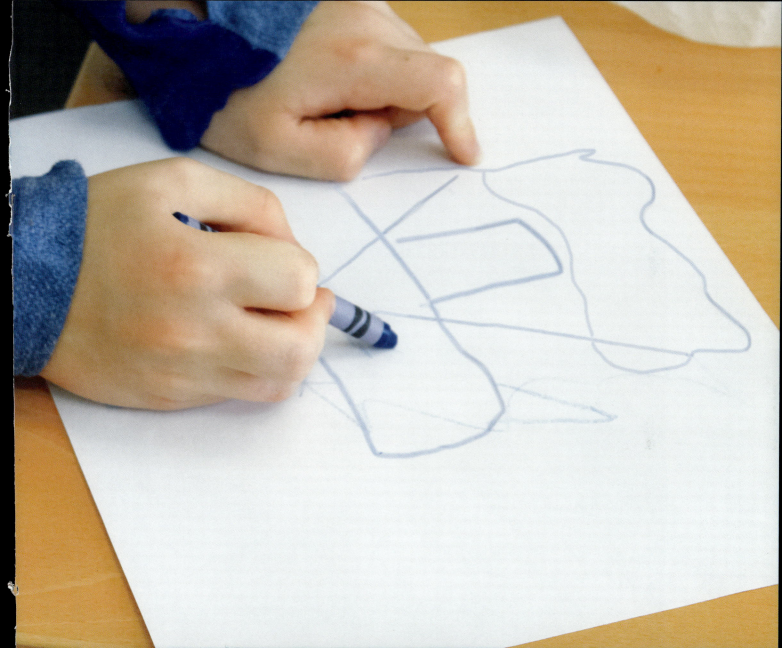

2. When you are ready to build your carrier, first decide how it will hold the egg. Will the egg rest in a box or a cup? Will you make your own structure out of materials such as straws?

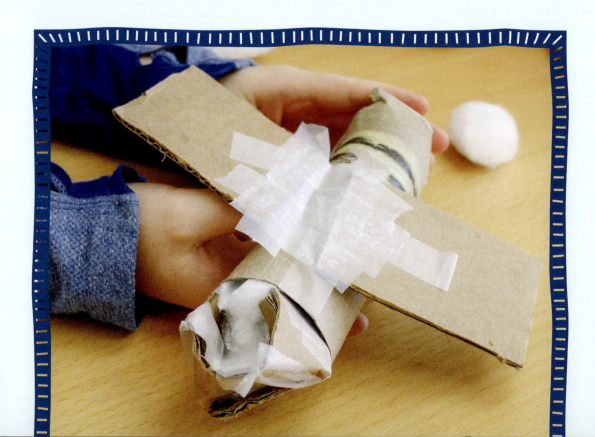

3. Choose your padding. Padding can include cotton balls or bubble wrap. Add your padding to the carrier. You can tape or glue it in place if you want it to stay put.

4. Attach any wings or parachutes to your carrier. These will increase drag.

5. Place your egg in the finished carrier. Remember that the tip of the egg can take the most impact force. How do you want to position your egg?

6. You can place a tarp or newspapers where you want to drop your egg. This will keep the ground cleaner if your egg breaks.

7. Drop your carrier. Start a few feet off the ground.

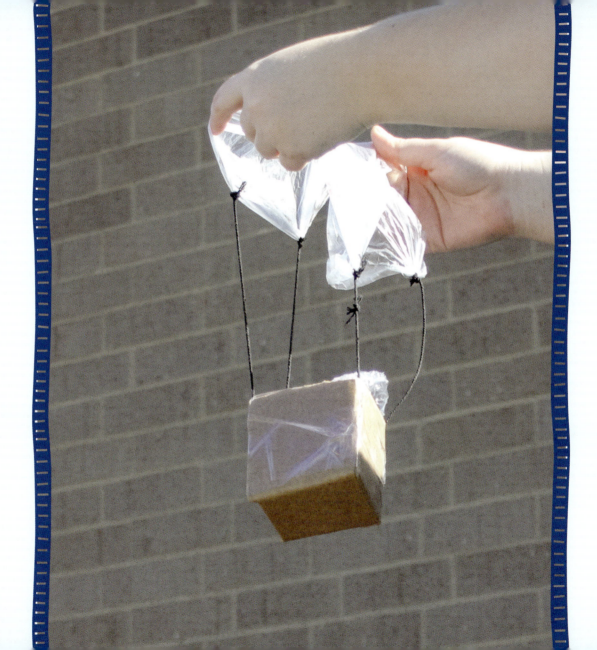

8. Check your egg for cracks or breaks. If the egg breaks, try again. Find ways to strengthen your carrier. If your egg makes the drop safely, drop it from a few feet higher. See if the egg survives the second drop.

9. Continue to raise the height of the drop. Ask an adult to drop your carrier from a high place. See how high you can drop your egg without it breaking!

Make It Better!

Congratulations! You have made a carrier to protect an egg. Now see if there are ways to improve it. Use any of these changes and see how they improve your carrier.

- You were given suggestions for materials to use to make your carrier. What else could you use to protect the egg?

- Not all types of ground are equally hard. Grass is softer than dirt or concrete. Does changing the type of ground make your egg more or less likely to break?

- Some egg drop competitions see who can use the fewest pieces to make a carrier. Can you use fewer pieces without breaking the egg?

Can you think of any ways that you could improve or change your carrier to make it better?

Glossary

brainstorm (BRAYN-storm): To come up with ideas.

collision (cuh-LI-zhun): When two or more objects crash together.

drag (DRAG): A force that pushes back on a falling object.

forces (FORSS-uhz): Pushes or pulls that change an object's movement.

gravity (GRA-vuh-tee): A force between two objects that attracts them to each other.

impact (IM-pakt): The force of one object hitting another.

kinetic energy (ki-NEH-tik EN-ur-jee): The energy of moving objects.

potential energy (puh-TEN-shuhl EN-ur-jee): The stored energy objects have due to their position.

surface area (SUR-fiss AYR-ee-uh): The space that covers the outside of an object.

velocity (vuh-LOSS-uh-tee): The speed of an object.

For More Information

Books

Alexa Kurzius. *Gravity*. New York, NY: Children's Press, 2019. This book explains what gravity is and how it interacts with objects and other forces.

Alison Eldridge and Stephen Eldridge. *Let's Experiment! The Scientific Method in the Lab*. New York, NY: PowerKids Press, 2020. This book teaches readers what the scientific method is and how to apply it to their experiments.

Daniel R. Faust. *Gravitational, Magnetic, and Electric Forces: Examining Interactions*. New York, NY: PowerKids Press, 2020. In this book, readers explore how gravitational, magnetic, and electric forces work in day-to-day life.

Websites

NASA Space Place: What Is Gravity? (https://spaceplace.nasa.gov/what-is-gravity/en/) This site describes the science behind gravity and how it affects life on Earth.

PBS Learning Media: Force and Motion (https://tpt.pbslearningmedia.org/resource/idptv11.sci.phys.maf.d4kfom/force-and-motion/) This video explains the three laws of motion and how objects react to a force being applied.

Wonderopolis: How Does a Parachute Work? (https://www.wonderopolis.org/wonder/how-does-a-parachute-work) Readers learn how parachutes work and the forces that act on them.

Index

About the Author

Katie Chanez is a children's book writer and editor originally from Iowa. She enjoys writing fiction, playing with her cat, and petting friendly dogs. Katie now lives and works in Minnesota.